Preface

Schubert received an important part of his early mu[sic]
at the Liechtental Parish Church, in the Vienna sub[urbs].
The composer's brother Ferdinand tells us that by h[is]
was first treble in the choir, and that he had also begun to compose 'small songs,
string quartets and piano pieces'. Michael Holzer, choirmaster at the Liechtental
church, taught him the rudiments of composition and said to him: 'Whenever I
wanted to impart something new to him, he always knew it already. I often
looked at him in silent wonder.'

It was a sympathetic milieu for the young composer, whose family were
themselves members of the Liechtental church, and after writing several shorter
liturgical works Schubert produced a complete Mass in F major for performance
there in 1814. A year later he composed the *Stabat Mater* in G minor. It is not
known whether it was commissioned, or written for a special occasion. It is
more likely that Schubert was, then as always, writing whatever he felt moved
to write – and if there was a good chance of performance, that was a bonus.
Perhaps the ancient devotional poem *Stabat Mater* had made a particular impact
on him during the celebrations of Holy Week, for it was eleven days after Good
Friday that he began work on his setting.

It took him three days to complete the work, which is for choir without
soloists, accompanied by a small orchestra. (His other setting of the *Stabat
Mater*, written only a year later – well *before* Good Friday 1816 – used
Klopstock's German version of the text and required soloists and a larger
orchestra.) Schubert sets only the first four three-line stanzas of the twenty-
stanza Latin poem, but having run through the three stanzas in sequence,
shaping them into a single broad musical strophe, he then repeats all three,
modifying his musical strophe with far-reaching variation that creates new
shades of intensity in the second stanza and extends the third to a fresh climax
of power and poignancy.

The inclusion of trombones – although there are no flutes, horns, trumpets, or
drums – is in keeping with an ecclesiastical tradition. It should be noted,
however, that Schubert originally intended to use horns; on the first page of the
autograph, 'Corni' is deleted and 'Tromboni' substituted. Due to technical
limitations, horns and trumpets in Schubert's day, unlike trombones, were
unable to produce many of the notes within their overall pitch-range. While
Schubert no doubt cherished the sonority of the trombones, he also valued their
greater usefulness in a minor key, and especially in the context of the chromatic
exploration we find in this *Stabat Mater*.

The present vocal score derives its vocal parts from the autograph full score kept
in the Wiener Stadt- und Landesbibliothek (shelf mark: MH 15/c). In this
respect the edition is an *Urtext*, the vocal parts being presented without
editorial amendments or additions, although accidentals superfluous to modern
requirements have been omitted tacitly. The new keyboard reduction is
designed for piano or organ. Where the bass line is given in octaves this
normally represents the composer's doubling of the cello line by the double
basses an octave lower. This effect, which is of course achieved on the organ by
using both 8' and 16' pedal stops, is an important element of the sonority
prescribed by the composer.

Brian Newbould
January 1989

Vorwort

Schubert erhielt einen wichtigen Teil seiner frühen Musikausbildung als Chorknabe der Gemeindekirche von Liechtental, dem Vorort von Wien, in dem seine Familie lebte. Ferdinand, der Bruder des Komponisten, berichtet, daß Franz mit elf Jahren (1807) erster Sopran des Chores war und begonnen hatte, kleine Lieder, Streichquartette und Klavierstücke zu komponieren. Michael Holzer, der Chormeister der Liechtentaler Kirche lehrte ihn die Grundzüge der Komposition und sagte über ihn: 'Wann auch immer ich ihn etwas Neues lehren wollte, wußte er es schon. Ich betrachtete ihn oft mit stiller Verwunderung.'

Ein verständnisvolles Milieu umgab den jungen Komponisten, dessen Familie selbst der Liechtentaler Kirche angehörte. Nachdem Schubert mehrere kürzere liturgische Werke geschrieben hatte, schuf er eine vollständige Messe in f-Dur, die 1814 dort aufgeführt wurde. Ein Jahr später komponierte er sein *Stabat Mater* in g-Moll. Es ist nicht bekannt, ob es als Auftragsarbeit oder für eine besondere Gelegenheit geschrieben wurde. Wahrscheinlicher ist jedoch, daß Schubert zu dem Zeitpunkt, wie auch später immer, daß schrieb, was er fühlte, schreiben zu müssen, und wenn er das Glück hatte, das er aufgeführt wurde, war das ein zusätzlicher Gewinn. Es ist möglich, daß das alte, andächtige Gedicht *Stabat Mater* während der Osterfeierlichkeiten in der Karwoche einen besonders tiefen Eindruck auf ihn gemacht hatte, denn es war elf Tage nach Karfreitag, daß er die Arbeit an diesem Satz begann.

Er brauchte drei Tage, um das Werk zu vollenden, welches für Chor ohne Solisten, begleitet von einem kleinen Orchester, gesetzt ist. (Seine andere Version von *Stabat Mater*, nur ein Jahr später, eine ganze Weile *vor* Karfreitag 1816, komponiert, legte Klopstocks deutsche Version des Textes zugrunde und verlangte Solisten und ein größeres Orchester.) Schubert vertonte nur die ersten vier dreizeiligen Strophen des zwanzig-strophigen lateinischen Gedichts, aber nach dem ersten Durchlauf der drei Strophen, die er in eine einzige große musikalische Strophe umformt, wiederholt er alle drei, wobei er sie durch weitausholende Variationen verändert und so in der zweiten Strophe bisher unbekannte Schattierungen der Intensität schafft und die dritte zu einem neuen Höhepunkt von Gewaltigkeit und bitterer Trauer bringt.

Die Einbeziehung von Posaunen – Flöten, Hörner, Trompeten oder Trommeln sind nicht vorhanden – entspricht einer kirchlichen Tradition. Es sollte jedoch erwähnt werden, daß Schubert ursprünglich Hörner verwenden wollte; auf der ersten Seite der Handschrift ist 'Corni' ausgestrichen und durch 'Tromboni' ersetzt. Jedoch anders als Posaunen, waren Hörner und Trompeten zu Schuberts Zeit aufgrund technischer Begrenzungen nicht in der Lage, viele der Noten ihres gesamten Tonbereiches zu produzieren. Schubert schätzte zweifellos die Klangfülle der Posaunen, aber er wußte ebenso ihre größere Verwendbarkeit für Moll-Tonarten zu würdigen, ganz besonders bei der chromatischen Erforschung, wie wir sie in diesem *Stabat Mater* finden.

Der vorliegende Klavierauszug bezieht seine Gesangsteile von der vollständigen Partitur der Urschrift, die sich in der Wiener Stadt- und Landesbibliothek (Signatur: MH 15/c) befindet. In dieser Hinsicht ist die Ausgabe ein *Urtext*, da die Stimmteile ohne herausgeberische Veränderungen und Zusätze vorgelegt werden, obwohl Vorzeichen, die für moderne Bedürfnisse überflüssig sind, stillschweigend weggelassen wurden. Das neue Arrangement für Tasteninstrumente ist für Klavier und Orgel entworfen. Wo die Baßmelodie in

FRANZ SCHUBERT

Stabat Mater

D.175

for SATB Chorus and Orchestra
für SATB Chor und Orchester

Edited · Herausgegeben von
Brian Newbould

Vocal score · Klavierauszug

FABER **ff** MUSIC

Orchestra

2 Oboes
2 Clarinets in B♭
2 Bassoons
3 Trombones
Organ
Strings

Duration *c.* 5 minutes
Spieldauer ca. 5 Minuten

Full score and parts are also available
Partitur und Stimmen sind ebenfalls erhältlich

This edition © 1989 by Faber Music Ltd
First published in 1989 by Faber Music Ltd
3 Queen Square London WC1N 3AU
Printed in England
Cover design by M & S Tucker
All rights reserved

Oktaven angegeben ist, entspricht das in der Regel der Wiederholung der Cellomelodie, durch den Kontrabaß eine Oktave tiefer im Satz des Komponisten. Dieser Effekt, der auf der Orgel natürlich durch die Pedalregister 8' und 16' erreicht wird, ist ein wichtiges Element der Klangfülle, die vom Komponisten vorgeschrieben ist.

Brian Newbould
Januar 1989
Deutsche Übersetzung: Helga Braun

Stabat mater dolorosa,
Juxta crucem lacrimosa,
Dum pendebat Filius.

Cujus animam gementem,
Contristatam, et dolentem,
Pertransivit gladius.

O quam tristis et afflicta,
Fuit illa benedicta,
Mater unigeniti!

Quae moerebat, et dolebat,
Pia Mater, dum videbat,
Nati poenas inclyti.

———

The mournful Mother stood
weeping beside the cross
while her son was hanging on it.

Her lamenting soul,
full of anguish and grief,
was pierced as by a sword.

Oh, how sad and distressed
was that blessed Mother
of an only son.

How she mourned and grieved,
that devoted Mother, as she watched
the suffering of her glorious son.

Die trauervolle Mutter stand
weinend neben dem Kreuz,
an dem der Sohn hing.

Ihre klagende Seele,
voller Schmerz und Trauer,
war von einem Schwert durchbohrt.

Oh, wie elend und gepeinigt
war diese gesegnete Mutter
des einzigen Sohnes.

Wie sie trauerte und litt
jene ergebene Mutter, als sie
das Leiden ihres glorreichen Sohnes mitansah.

Stabat Mater

Edited by
Brian Newbould

Franz Schubert
D. 175

Lyrics (mm. 5–): Sta - bat ma - ter — do - lo - ro - sa jux - ta

et af - flic - ta fu - it il - la

et ____ af - flic - ta fu - it il - la

et af - flic - ta fu - it il - la

et af - flic - ta fu - it il - la

be - ne - dic - ta ma - ter u - ni - ge - ni -

be - ne - dic - ta ma - ter u - ni - ge - ni -

be - ne - dic - ta ma - ter u - ni - ge - ni -

be - ne - dic - ta ma - ter u - ni - ge - ni -

-de - bat na - ti poe - nas in - cly - ti.

-de - bat na - ti poe - nas in - cly - ti.

-de - bat na - ti poe - nas in - cly - ti.

dum vi - de - bat poe - nas in - cly - ti.

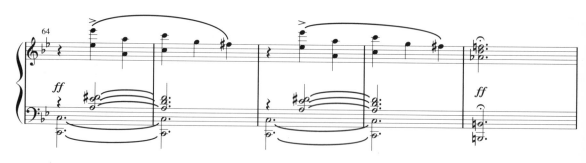

-de - bat Fi - li - us,

-de - bat Fi - li - us,

-de - bat Fi - li - us,

-de - bat Fi - li - us,

cu - jus a - ni-mam ge - men - tem, con - tris -

cu - jus a - ni-mam ge - men - tem, con - tris -

cu - jus a - ni-mam ge - men - tem, con - tris -

cu - jus a - ni - mam ge - men - tem, con - tris -

14

in - cly - ti.

in - cly - ti.

in - cly - ti.

in - cly - ti.

Faber Motet Series

Rome, Seville, Lisbon, Venice or Prague—cities whose music, architecture, art and history cannot fail to captivate. Faber Music's Motet Series draws upon the musical heritage of these five cities, resulting in powerfully evocative collections of 16th- and 17th-century motets by the leading composers at that time. Some of these works were previously unpublished, and all were hitherto unavailable in good modern editions. The city theme for each publication gives historical and geographical unity to the collections, thereby offering invaluable concert programming possibilities to choirs. There are also informative introductions, which provide historical context, and translations of the texts for reference.

Masterworks from Rome *edited by Graham Dixon*   ISBN 0-571-51260-7

Rome, centre of the Western Church and a focus of musical excellence in the Renaissance, played host to many of the leading Italian church composers of the day, including Festa, Marenzio and the musical giant, Palestrina. However, Rome was a truly cosmopolitan centre, and so this collection of nine motets also draws on works from Spanish composers such as Morales and Victoria, who both worked in Rome for a period of time, and Northerners such as Desprez and Arcadelt, who both sang in the Papal choir.

Masterworks from Lisbon *edited by Ivan Moody*   ISBN 0-571-51603-3

With a rich combination of musical influences from both Portugal and Spain, Lisbon stood at a cultural crossroads in the 17th century. The diversity of this cosmopolitan centre is captured here in a superb collection of eight works by composers such as Duarte Lôbo, Cardoso, Correia, Guerrero and Morales.

Masterworks from Seville *edited by Tess Knighton*   ISBN 0-571-51652-1

As the gateway to the New World, Seville's relative wealth and cultural mix has long supported a colourful, vibrant atmosphere. The rich musical life of the city, with the cathedral as its focal point, reached its apogee in the Renaissance and this collection presents ten outstanding choral works by the leading figures of the day, including Pedro and Francisco Guerrero, Morales, Escobar and Ceballos.

Masterworks from Venice *edited by Jerome Roche*   ISBN 0-571-51286-0

The importance of Venice in the 16th and 17th centuries hardly needs emphasizing here, and in many ways this collection of eight motets represents some of the most well-known composers in the Renaissance and Baroque eras; figures such as Andrea Gabrieli, Willaert and Monteverdi. In fact, all bar one of the composers included here were employed at the basilica of S. Marco at some point in their careers, providing a wonderful coherence to the collection.

Masterworks from Prague *edited by Noel O'Regan*   ISBN 0-571-51884-2

In 1576 Prague became the capital of the vast Hapsburg kingdom when the Emperor Rudolf II moved his splendid court to the Hradschin Castle and the gothic cathedral of St Veit. It was to become a melting pot of prodigious artistic and scientific talent. Some of the period's richest musical treasures are presented in this collection of eleven works by de Kerle, Regnart, Gallus and de Monte; motets for the main feasts of the church year are included as well as Gallus's famous Holy Week motet, *Ecce quomodo moritur*, traditionally sung in Lutheran Germany after the Bach *Passions*.